THE PLIGHT OF THE MARTYR
dying on unnecessary hills

EMILY OAKLEY

The Plight of the Martyr
Dying on Unnecessary Hills
By Emily R. Oakley

Published by RB Publications
Wichita, Kansas USA

Rebirth Ministries Inc.
3810 N. Walker Avenue
Maize, Kansas 67101
USA

www.rebirthmin.com

ISBN: 978-0-578-85972-9

Library of Congress Control Number: 2021903153

Also available in eBook format.

Third Printing.

DEDICATION

To my Savior, who has never once given up on me and teaches me more and more about His love and grace. And to the best family and friends a woman could ask for. Thanks for always believing in me and for challenging me to be more than I ever thought I could be.

CONTENTS

PREFACE

I believe some of the greatest lessons in life come out of personal experience, and this book is chock full of those experiences for me. We all have our shortcomings, and we all face different obstacles. It is my hope that this book will help tackle one of those obstacles, unnecessary martyrdom. As we journey together, I hope that I can either help you or help you assist someone else who may struggle with dying on hills that are never meant to be died on. I hope it will help people understand that there are some things that are worth the fight, and there are many others that need to be constantly surrendered to Jesus.

I struggled to write this book, and I believe a large part of that is because I have just recently come to the understanding of what it means to climb down these hills and not become a martyr to things Jesus never asked of me. For me, writing is a therapeutic experience of looking back at the lessons I have recently learned and being grateful to never have to die on another hill again. This book would not have happened without wonderful people in my life pointing me to the loving arms of my Savior and showing me the blind spots I had missed in myself. Even though I have been a therapist for a few years now, there were blind spots in my own life that I was missing, and I am thankful to have people who continue to love me and guide me through obstacles.

As we go through the journey of climbing on and off the hill(s) of martyrdom, I pray that you will hear the welcoming voice of the Savior beckoning you into His arms of freedom and peace. I pray that we will understand that we spend way too much of our lives focused on things that are never meant to take up our focus and that life is much simpler when we keep our gaze fixed upon Jesus. As we go through these pages together, allow the Holy Spirit to prompt your heart toward further consideration, and ask that He shine light on blind spots in your own life. May we learn how to lay down our unnecessary martyrdom so that we can pick up true and eternal freedom in Christ.

Blessings,
Emily

CHAPTER ONE
the base of the hill

This book comes at the suggestion of a good friend who has been a part of the ups and downs of my journey in recent years. I cannot take credit for the title because God gave it to him, and he thinks I would be the perfect candidate to pen the pages. Why? Because I have been the queen of dying on unnecessary hills and being an unnecessary martyr. I have spent most of my life worrying about what people would think and who I would offend, and have often "sacrificed" myself at the altar of opinion. If I may be frank, it has been quite exhausting.

While martyrdom is often considered admirable, the kind of martyr I became is not one worth celebrating. When I think of great martyrs, I think about the apostles:

Paul, Peter, James, and others. These are men who died for a worthy and noble cause they believed in, the Gospel of Jesus Christ. In Scripture, we see them experience a true transformation and become willing to die for a life that has brought them healing, wholeness and a place of belonging. The cause I was dying for (and can sometimes still fall into the trap of) is the good graces of others. I have spent countless hours worrying about who I was offending, how to fix it, and what would happen if they ended up hating me for the rest of my life. I can fight battles that are not mine to fight and spend hours on a hill that God never intended for me to be on. While we should be mindful of how we are treating people, I let possible outcomes and reactions consume me.

Martyrdom, though, is not just limited to circumstances relating to people. For others, it might be tasks and just HAVING to accomplish the next thing or pour our entire lives into our work. We can sometimes fall into the trap of dying on the altar of business. These examples of being martyrs at the altar of tasks or the opinions of others are not the only examples of unnecessary martyrdom we can look to, but they are just two of the many. (Please feel free to insert your own area where you are unnecessarily dying on a hill as we go through these pages together.)

I did not start at the top of the hill of unnecessary martyrdom, and I do not believe any of the rest of us do, either. This was not a parachuting experience where I jumped from the plane and landed on top and just ran with it. This was a slow climb with lots of valleys and hills. I have had seasons when I have done okay and seasons when I have done terribly. However, while most of life is about climbing to reach new successes, climbing up this particular hill led to anything but a successful outcome. In fact, getting back off this hill of martyrdom is not only a kind suggestion but vital to successful Christian living.

Allow me the opportunity to switch gears here just a little bit. If you think about warfare, the best vantage point is the high ground. You can see all around and get a better idea of where the enemy is. However, at the top of a hill, you also have nowhere else to run. (Think of the very top peak of a hill where there is no sideways mobility.) When you are on the ground level, you have a lot more ground to traverse, so if you are trying to fight a battle up on a hill by yourself, your chances of success are much smaller. The army below is not going anywhere, and, if you are like me, you can be stuck just swinging your sword to your heart's content until you are too tired and worn out to do anything else about it. This is all happening while swinging aimlessly and hitting nothing. And, let me tell you, I have spent much of my young adult life very tired. Battles are meant to be fought where there is the optimal advantage, not stuck in one place with nowhere to turn. Battles are also not meant to be fought alone. Though it is easier to pick off enemies from the higher vantage point, one's chance of success while fighting an entire battle alone while swarms of enemies are coming is slim.

If you are fighting the Lord's battle, you are not doing it alone. Fighting the unnecessary battle of self-imposed martyrdom, however, is not only without the Lord's blessing, it is completely unsuccessful. In Acts 6, the disciples were recognizing a gap and understanding that they could not meet every need in the church and community. Some of them were called to preach the Word, yet there were other duties needing to be performed within the church. Reflect on this quote from Acts 6:2-4:

> "And the twelve summoned the full number of the disciples and said, 'It is not right that we should give up preaching the word of God to serve tables.

Therefore, brothers, pick out from among you seven men of good repute, full of the Spirit and of wisdom, whom we will appoint to this duty. But we will devote ourselves to prayer and to the ministry of the word.'"

The disciples recognized that the needs of the early church were growing, but they had wisdom enough to recognize that they could not do it all.

Again, I am speaking to you from the VERY personal experience of having taken on too much at times. Some causes are absolutely worth fighting for. Scripture, as in James 1:27, tells us that we are to fight for those who cannot fight for themselves, for justice, for the poor, the widow, the orphan, and more. However, if we fight to constantly try and attain the applause of others or to try to fix the things God did not ask us to try to fix, we not only wear ourselves out but can also be a detriment to the process the Holy Spirit is trying to work out. If we try to be the ones to complete every task or feel like we have to keep striving toward the next goal, we can miss what God wants to do in us in the very present moment. Sometimes, God wants to use others, and it is okay if He chooses to use someone else instead of us. We are not meant to do all the things, and, far too often, we try to do just that.

At the base of my individual hill (and, I am sure, yours as well) is Fort Good Intentions. This is where my "plight" begins. Yours may look different or have a different journey, but hopefully my example can be relevant for you as well. Being a Christ-follower, we want to be kind, and we want others to see Jesus when we live out our day-to-day lives. My Fort is full of wanting the best outcomes and just wanting to be as kind and loving as possible. However, it is very easy to get our eyes off the commander (Jesus) and onto the other members of the army whom we want to please or help fix. When I have ended up on unnecessary hills, it has not only left me worn out, but I do not end up being as kind or as loving as Jesus has asked me to be because I have taken on a burden I was never meant to fix or carry.

Being a counselor has been a very ironic job for me, in that it is a career where I can fix no one. People do not come to my office because I can change them (though many believe that is the job of a counselor); people come to my office so that I can ask them insightful questions and help them on their path of self-discovery. Too often, we try to put on the battle armor meant for others and run on the path they were meant to run. What happens? We look like crazy people with disjointed metal clanging together. Even King David knew he could not use King Saul's armor, though it was given to him to wear. It did not fit him and actually would have kept him from fulfilling God's purpose for Him. (This delightful story is found in 1 Samuel 17.) What can we learn from this? Wear the armor you are meant to wear; stay in the lane God designs for you to be in. You are not supposed to be anyone else or serving anyone else's purpose.

We cannot please everyone, and we can fix no one. Humans are not meant to fix other humans; that is God's job. Can we affect change? You bet. Can we change the hearts of others? No, we cannot. So, what happens? We exhaust hours of our lives on causes we should not fight. We take our eyes off Kingdom purposes and put them on earthly or personal achievements. While these things are not bad on their own, they hinder us when they take our eyes away from Jesus. On the same note, we cannot complete every task in the entire world. We are not meant to do everything everyone asks us to do. Our entire lives are not meant to be about work. Of course, I understand that all of this is much easier said than done. While we all have tasks to accomplish in life, the hill of accomplishing everything and running at a breakneck pace with no rest is also not the way God designed us.

All our personalities and ways that God made us are meant to be used for good in the Kingdom. However, because of sin and the brokenness of the world, there are fragmented parts of our personalities that can lead to unnecessary heartaches like martyrdom. We will discuss this more in detail later, but be aware of who you are. I do not just mean this in the simplistic sense of the activities you enjoy doing or your favorite food or color, but really take a moment to get honest with yourself and allow the Holy Spirit to illuminate the parts of you that are not operating in the exact way God has created you to be.

So, here we are at the bottom of the hill with the best of intentions in the world. We want to serve, and we want to love, but do we allow this to be something that drives us instead of the will God has for us? As we journey through this book, we will see how even the best of intentions can distract us from where our eyes should be focused. We all want to sacrifice and live for worthy causes, but I just wonder if some of our causes are only worthy through worldly eyes. If they are godly causes, do we take on more than the Lord has asked us to take on? Do we bear a load He is wanting us to lay down, not to die for? Join me as we take a look at the journey of becoming and releasing unnecessary martyrdom. How does any journey up begin? Generally with a slow climb.

THE PLIGHT OF THE MARTYR

CHAPTER TWO
the slow climb

As I alluded to in the previous chapter, becoming a full-fledged unholy (as in God-did-not-ask-it-of-us) martyr does not just happen overnight. It takes countless hours and badly-wired thought patterns before fully entering this very destructive lifestyle and cycle. And, as mentioned, it starts at Fort Good Intentions. For me, this journey has been present from a very early age. Let me elaborate on what this Fort looks like and how it comes to be. Again, as I share my own experiences, please allow the Holy Spirit to speak to you about how the stories and circumstances in your life can apply.

My mom tells me that I have been a helper in whatever capacity I could be since I could walk. I wanted to help her clean up or help with my brother (even if my help was not always very helpful), but I constantly wanted to please. From a young age, I have hated disappointing people, and I went to extraordinary lengths to do anything I could to make them happy. Being a helper is a wonderful trait, but it quickly became the sole thing my worth and identity were wrapped up in. I only found value from the eyes of other people, not the eyes of Jesus.

I can remember a time back in elementary school when I said some not nice words to a fellow classmate. This particular girl had really made me mad, and, in my fourth-grade lack of maturity, I responded accordingly. When my teacher caught wind of it and (rightfully) disciplined me, I was a mess. I had disappointed my teacher and not just any teacher, a teacher I deeply respected and loved. Of course, I apologized immediately and desperately wanted to do anything I could to make it right. There were consequences at school, and then I continued with the rest of my day in agony and overwhelming disappointment in myself. I remember going home just so defeated and angry for not only disappointing myself but also disappointing this teacher. I remember my mom, in all her loving kindness, telling me that I had done enough punishing of myself and there would be no further action taken. My mom had grace for me, and I am thankful that she did. Should I have had remorse for my actions? Yes. My parents disciplined me when I made poor choices, but, in that moment, my mom was wise enough to see that I had already inflicted enough pain on myself. Remorse does not equate to beating ourselves down to a pulp, but it does help us change, learn the lesson and move forward. I have not always been very good at the moving forward part.

Elementary school Emily kept that same mentality and continued to sacrifice herself at the altar of others. When I was twelve, it then turned into very unhealthy codependency (which is a whole other topic for a whole other book, but basically means all your emotional eggs are tied into one other person's basket) and spiraled into a very dark habit. However, it did not start out that way. It started with me wanting to be kind to others. It started with me wanting to consider the hearts and opinions of others. It started with me wanting to help. While this in and of itself is not wrong, it quickly got out of hand because I took my eyes off Jesus in the process. I will be completely honest and say that people became my idol because they were, most regrettably, what I worshipped. I had forgotten that as long as my heart and mind were centered on Christ, everything else would fade away and not become center stage in the unhealthy play I had written for myself.

As a follower of Christ, I am instructed to be kind and empathetic to others. I am taught that grace and compassion are paramount and that truth given without love can be counterproductive to the transformation process. However, this does not mean that I am meant to be trampled on in the name of others' emotions. The young girl from elementary school grew up to be someone who put way too much of her identity and value in life into making sure other people were happy, as has been alluded to previously. I climbed hill after hill trying to make everyone happy, and, all the while, I was endlessly wearing myself out.

Care and consideration are important, but not everyone will agree with us all the time. There is no way to make everyone happy 24/7. Even the perfect Son of Man, Jesus, does not make everyone happy, because what He has to say is controversial and opposite of the way people expect things to be. What Jesus is saying is 100% truth, and not everyone likes what He has to say, because it goes against their ideals. If people cannot always accept the perfect truth of Christ, how will we fare in always making others happy? We will not fare well. We will all make mistakes. No one, other than Jesus, is perfect (sorry if that bursts your bubble), and we will all have to own up to the mistakes we make. We do not handle others carelessly, but we do understand that it is our responsibility to live biblically, not spending our lives coddling.

Care and consideration also do not mean that we say yes to everything everyone asks us to do or to every task that comes our way, as we read from Acts 6. Wanting to help others and execute details with excellence are important, but I have seen too many individuals sacrifice their own selfcare to tasks and endless responsibilities. Obviously, responsibility is a part of life, but we cannot properly care for the tasks God wants us to care for if we are constantly burning the candle at both ends. Both dying for the opinions of others and dying for the endless tasks of others are counterproductive.

As can probably be inferred from the previous points of discussion in this book, part of the struggle in dealing with my plight comes when I spend too much time focusing on other people instead of God. A self-imposed martyr spends a lot of sideways energy looking at everything that cannot be fixed or all the tasks that need to be done and ignores the one place that can transform and offer peace in the midst of the ever-chaotic world, the presence of Jesus. Life is much simpler if all that wasted energy spent worrying about other people or the never-ending to-do list shifts into something productive, into time with God. This investment will never return void. If a truly transformative experience happens as we encounter Jesus on a daily basis and let Him renew us from the inside out, we do not have to worry about whether or not we are offending people or getting everything done, because we will be too busy focusing on trying to walk in the God-given purpose we were meant to have. It will help us narrow our scope to accomplishing the goals that He has for us, not the ones we feel we need to take on. It will help us serve others around us as He instructs us to support them.

Allow me to expand just a little further on the idea of never-ending tasks. I believe there is this idea that we are meant to be ridiculously busy at all times in order to be successful in the Kingdom. Resting is optional instead of necessary. We are taught to be the "yes" people and do everything that comes our way, because saying no is not an option, so it can be easy to throw ourselves into all the tasks. While it is important to do our work and do it to the best of our ability, I wonder how many hills of busyness are climbed unnecessarily. I wonder how many "yeses" were meant to be "nos." I am by no means suggesting laziness or lack of discipline. Obviously, we all have tasks to accomplish and work to be done. I just wonder how much of it is work that God asks us to do and how much is work we feel we MUST do. Have you ever seen a professional juggler? Now, some of these guys are insane and can juggle multiple objects for long periods of time. Inevitably, though, juggling all those objects cannot be done forever. The talented individual either stops, or, eventually, like we regular humans who stink at juggling, something drops. Regardless, juggling items Jesus does not ask us to juggle throws off the balance and takes our eyes off the important work we need to do.

What if you have died at the altar of your work or attempted to juggle too many items at one time? This is a relatable area for a lot of people, including people in ministry. While a lot of our work is done with the good intentions of Kingdom purpose, sometimes we take on things God flatly did not ask us to take on. We want to serve in every manner capable or be a blessing to those around us. While those are all noble causes, we can burn out fast, and I have seen this happen on more than one occasion. We are never meant to be martyrs to activity, but, more often than not, our focus can shift from Kingdom work to how we find earthly value. There is a problem when we find more validation in the work of our hands than in the words of our Savior. Again, doing tasks and doing them with excellence is honoring and biblical. I am just reminding us that nothing defines us outside of our Savior. This includes people or tasks.

Once enough time passes for the culmination of all the moments of martyrdom, we realize we are at the top of a hill that we really had no intention of being on. The air is a lot thinner, and the ability to process and think clearly all but evaporates. Putting our eyes on everything external can often keep us from missing that good work that God wants to do in the internal.

While the choice to be calm and reassess the path to the bottom seems to be the most logical one, it is not often the most commonly made. And, when getting off the hill of martyrdom, you cannot go down the same way you came up; in fact, you must find an entirely different path altogether. So, what do people naturally do when they get to a place where they are stuck and do not know how to get back down? They panic. And they panic badly.

THE PLIGHT OF THE MARTYR

CHAPTER THREE
panic from the top

Have you ever watched any of those Mt. Everest-type movies that go horribly wrong? People get stuck at the top of the mountain in the middle of a terrible storm with no way back down and no way to communicate with the people down below. Someone's rope breaks, or some other cataclysmic experience transpires, and getting back down takes a lot of time and heartache. Sometimes, people do not make it back down at all. Being at the top of Mt. Martyrdom can also elicit the same reactions and fears. If we allow ourselves to be on the top of this mountain, we will experience heartache and pain and lose much valuable time.

When I first realized the mess I had gotten myself into, I will not lie, I panicked. While I knew this was a not a biblical response, it was very much the one that was triggered in my humanity. Climbing this particular hill had taken me years, and I had no idea how I was going to get back down at a faster rate than I had gotten up. There were many tears and many moments of genuine concern that I was not going to be able to do this. When you realize that you are at the top, it can be really overwhelming. You may ask yourself, "How do I move forward? What are the next steps to becoming the person God has created me to be? How do I let go of that which I am not supposed to hold onto? I have read all these thousands of Scriptures, like Proverbs 15:18, about not being subject to my feelings or letting these outside forces dictate my life, but here I am, being a martyr to all the wrong causes. How, oh, God, do I get myself off this hill?"

It is normal for humans to have moments of uncertainty; just read the Scriptures about men such as Doubting Thomas, who did not believe Jesus had been raised from the dead (John 20:24-25). But, you cannot get off the hill until you acknowledge how you got yourself there in the first place, and this takes time and self-awareness that many individuals do not have. In some cases, this is awareness that individuals do not want to have. Getting to this place of self-awareness takes brutal and honest conversations with others and yourself about the areas of your life that may have shortcomings, and it also requires action and change. Often, this is not something a lot of people want to do.

My martyrdom looks like pleasing other people and wanting to be in control of everything all around me, but your martyrdom may look like our discussions of tasks or something else entirely. The beauty of allowing other people to speak into our lives is that they often have a different vantage point. Whatever the hill, it is important to consider if this is really a hill you are meant to die on. Does this further the expansion of Kingdom purpose or add fuel to the fire of unnecessary struggle? Does God really want me to feel discouraged, lost, panicked, or without a general sense of victory in my life?

When you get real with yourself, there is often a moment of "Oh, no! What in the world have I done?" You can begin replaying countless situations or beating yourself up because this is not the goal or mountain you ever intended to find yourself on, yet it is the point you have reached all the same. We all have moments of chaos, but too often we live fueled by the panic instead of by the peace. Every one of us is subject to our flesh, and panic is one of the ways that can pan out. If God can repeatedly save Israel from themselves, He can certainly do it for us as well, as long as we are willing to let go and let Him have the reins in our lives.

When people come into my office for counseling, they are often in one of two places: panic or despair. Something either triggers an immediate response of "This should not be this way," or "I have been here so long, I do not know how to get out; I recognize that there is a problem, but how in the world do I make progress?" It is my job to sit with them at this place in their journey. Thankfully, Christ meets us in these moments as well. While our loving Heavenly Father understands our natural human inclinations, He is loving enough to tell us this is not a place we have to stay. We might be in panic, but we are not stuck there. We get the choice to change.

When people panic, they can operate in a couple of different modes. (I hate scary movies and refuse to watch them, but over the course of my life, I have seen a couple.) Anytime something scary happens or there is a threatening figure lurking about, the characters make one of two choices: they fight, or they flee. (Sometimes they freeze, but that is not fitting for the purpose of this particular analogy.) You scream at the television, "Get going! Move faster! You are never going to make it!" However, no matter how much one may try to encourage the fictitious character who cannot hear you through the television, the reality does not seem to change. Hollywood drama loves a good suspense story, and those of us watching can see so clearly how these characters can avoid a bad outcome. What of this is also true in our Christian lives? Often, I have wondered if I had blocked God's voice from trying to tell me to "Get going" or to avoid the hill I was trying to climb. Much like the fictitious character on the television, how many times have God's warnings to me fallen on deaf ears? The humbling reality is that this occurs much more often than I would like to admit.

Once we realize we are in a scary or very unpleasant situation, the human brain can digress into a state of panic, which, in turn, causes our brains to move into toxic stress. We do not engage our brains in the process they were meant to be engaged in, and we deter our moments of healing and health when we allow our thoughts to become chaotic and our lives to be ruled by panic. Panic is also learned, contrary to popular belief. Any negative response we have in life is one that we learn, not one that is automatically in our brains.

Maybe your panic is much more internal, and you just look at the world around you and feel completely overwhelmed, wondering how in the world you will get yourself out of the mess you are in. No matter what it may look like for you, there is often the realization that where you are is not any place you truly want to be. And that, my friend, is okay. We all have those moments; we just now get the beautiful choice to decide what it is that we do with them.

Eventually, we can arrive at a place where we no longer panic or feel overwhelmed but take a moment to assess the situation. We can look around and have a moment of honesty with ourselves. We can acknowledge the unnecessary plight we are in. Then, and only then, with the help of Jesus, can we continue to make the necessary forward progress.

CHAPTER FOUR
acknowledgment of the plight

Self-awareness is a huge part of acknowledging the plight of being a martyr. If we ignore how we think and process or the worldview out of which we operate, it will be much harder to recognize when there is a problem. Knowing ourselves and how we operate is vital to success, and it may shock us to know that most people are not as aware of themselves as one might think. If our self-awareness has blind spots, or we are unsure of these areas, it is most helpful to ask a trusted friend or family member who can provide insight into what we are missing. We are meant to be a body of believers for many reasons, and one of those reasons includes lovingly helping one another when there are things we may not see.

In life, it can be easy to fall into the "what-if" trap:

What if I had chosen a different path? What if I had not let that moment affect me? What if I had made a different choice? What if? The danger in these statements is that not a single thing can be done about what has already happened. We cannot change past or sometimes even present circumstances. Honestly, there is not a whole lot in life we can control or change other than ourselves. We cannot change what we have done, but we can acknowledge the reality of what is so that we can move forward, not making the same mistakes. It is very hard to acknowledge anything if we do not acknowledge current reality and the steps that we took to get there. "What is" truly remains the only malleable piece of the puzzle when the acknowledgement of the plight has set in. Recognizing what Jesus wants to change in us helps us continue moving past those what-if moments.

During one of my seasons of being an unnecessary martyr (the number of these seasons that I have had can often be hard to count), God was faithful and loving enough to show me different visions of how much I was making a small problem a much bigger deal than necessary.

Imagine with me a brunette woman, early thirties, average height, dressed in oversized body armor like a knight would wear. If that picture is not enough to make you laugh, I do not know what is. When I saw myself in this armor, it definitely felt like one of the King David moments I was speaking of earlier, someone wearing a suit of armor not intended for them. It was clanky and bulky, and a clumsy person such as myself needs no further help in potential trip-ups. Once I had seen the armor I was never mean to wear, God took me to a battle scene full of lots of loud noise and crazy commotion all around. I had a very large sword in my hand, and I was swinging with all my might at the seemingly monstrous problems looming all around. Then, I heard a gentle voice telling me to hand over my sword. As I recognized this to be the voice of God, I faced a panicked decision of walking away from something I felt was mine to fight and choosing obedience. Again, I heard the Lord: "Emily, this is not your battle to fight. Hand me the sword and go over there." Over there was a beach with a chair and a sign that read "Peace."

As I reluctantly handed my sword over to God and began walking toward the beach, I realized that in my other hand was a magnifying glass. I had made a problem that was small in the eyes of God something very big. However, when I took the magnifying glass away, it was easy to see it as something not worth my energy and effort. As I looked back toward the scene of the battle, I could no longer hear or see it going on. All I saw was the presence of God like a forcefield shielding the area, blocking out the noise and fighting the battle I was not meant to fight. When we are martyrs, it can be far too easy to get wrapped up in battles that do not have Kingdom purpose. It can be easy to want to get engulfed in something that was not even meant to be fixed by anyone other than God. We can walk around with swords we were never meant to carry.

Why, then, is it so hard to let go of the battles we fight? Because there is a deep need for human control that all of us experience at one time or another. We hate uncertainty and unknown variables, and we do not like when the thoughts we have for our lives do not go as planned. I believe that some of us have a more controlling personality by nature than others, but this does not mean that we do not want to have the reins on our lives. Often, taking those reins can lead to disastrous results. For me, my control obsession leads to fighting battles that God has never asked me to fight. It leads me to trying to control variables that were never mine to control. It leads to a hard season of having absolutely no peace, and this is no one's responsibility but my own. Thankfully, most of this hardship is no longer a part of my life. Praise God for His faithfulness, goodness and mercy!

While my intentions are mostly pure (I will be honest and say there have been far more moments than I like to admit when I have done things out of selfishness), there are some battles that are just not meant for me to fight. There are causes in the world worth fighting for (I have alluded to some of those earlier), but trying to fix people, situations or singlehandedly trying to accomplish all of life's goals is going to leave us perpetually tired and disappointed in our results. We are part of the army of God, but we are not the Commander-in-Chief. It is not ours to come up with battle strategy. The job of being Commander-in-Chief and strategizing the best plans belongs to God. It is a much more peaceful state of being when we recognize that right away instead of waiting until after we have sweat to death in armor while holding a sword we were never meant to carry. There were never meant to be two leaders. Our lives can get really clunky when we try to walk in the role that belongs to Jesus. What is God asking you to put down today? What is He asking you to let go? I encourage you to take a moment to let the

Holy Spirit talk to you about some of the specific swords you need to hand over.

As another sidenote, not everything everyone deals with has to do with us. While the pain of other people may come our direction or be projected onto us, we cannot be so blind as to think it all has to do with us. Martyrs take everything anyone says, or the removal of a task, and apply it too personally. They can often adopt the victim mentality. How do I know this? Because I have, unfortunately, been a champ at making it all about me. As I sit here and write these pages, lessons of my past flood my mind with encouragement from a loving God who helps me move past those hurdles as well as present and future ones.

We can also make it all about ourselves when we are executing Kingdom work. God does not need us to make sure every task in the whole world gets completed nor need us to say yes to every opportunity that comes our way. I know I mentioned this earlier in the book, but I believe it is an important concept to really hammer home. The Kingdom of God was here before us, and it will be here after us, with other people being used of the Lord. Even though God wants to use us, He does not HAVE to have us to get His purposes accomplished. I, for one, am thankful for that, as we humans have a tendency to try and mess things up when we do them on our own. While we may understand this in word, it is much different to execute this in deed.

The enemy wants us to spend our lives feeling like victims: victims of society, of the church, of other people, of our circumstances, of feelings, of our to-do lists, and on and on this list goes. Martyrs are not exempt from this mentality. We can be victims of the perception of others, our unending to-do list or assumptions that may or may not be true. Assumptions are one of the biggest ways we can make our lives much more difficult than they need to be. We can also be victims of not having enough time in the day to get everything done. In any of these moments, we do not have to be victims of anything. In fact, Jesus designs us to be the exact opposite; He designs us to be victorious.

I also feel as though I need to share another hard truth: We become martyrs when we become our own gods. Whatever in the world could I mean by that? Well, being an unholy martyr comes when we look to ourselves to be the lord of our lives instead of looking to THE Lord of all life.

We do not die on unnecessary hills by looking to God to be the One who is in charge. We trust that He knows what is best, and we can only do that when we lay down our self-idolatry. On our own, we are hot messes; with Christ, and only with Christ, we are victorious. Allie Beth Stuckey offers a beautiful perspective on the danger of trying to be our own gods and live through our own strength in her book, *You're Not Enough (And That's Okay)*. I believe reading this book will help in the journey of releasing martyrdom.

When the moment of clarity arrives that God did not design us to live on these hills, to be our own god, or to be victims to projected pain, momentary difficulty, an unending to-do list, or every opportunity we feel we must be a part of, we can then begin to see our hills through a new lens of hope. We can acknowledge that trying to be our own god leads us nowhere good really, really fast. We may still be stuck at the top, but now the difference is that we can see we are at a destination that was never meant to be the ending point of the journey. We can see that things from up high can be really daunting, but there is peace waiting at the base of the mountain. We can let God be the only God in our lives as we look to serving Him instead of ourselves. Climbing back down from the top of the hill requires the acknowledgement of where we are and how we got here and acknowledgment that this is a place we do not want to be. So, now, how do we move forward? Allow me yet again to share a personal experience.

I remember the time in my life when I realized the hill I had arrived on. Though this was not my first hill of martyrdom, it was the first time I had understood how I had allowed myself to get to this place and why I kept ending up in this very destructive pattern. Perpetual martyrs will go from hill to hill based on the circumstance or situation in their lives. Sometimes, the hill explodes (and I do mean explodes), and they are forced to keep moving in search of the next unnecessary hill to die on. Sometimes, they move to another hill and continue on the same trajectory of destructive choices. This time, for me, the choice had been made to climb down from the hill and not get back onto another one that did not have Kingdom purpose and eternal value. For all of us martyrs out there, we start moving forward by making the decision that we want to change where we are.

It was in the recent past that I was able to really acknowledge that I truly had a problem with carrying weight and climbing on hills that were not my burden. And, as I looked back down on a hill that I had familiarized myself with, I began a process of recognizing and understanding how I had gotten myself there in the first place. I began to understand that my identity had not been consumed by the perfect and unending love of God the Father, but, rather, it had been consumed by the identity of myself in the eyes of other people (or what I thought other people might think). I could almost see the notches carved out on the hill as I had made on my ascent to where I had landed: notch one, worrying about the opinions of others; notch two worrying whether I had offended others; notch three and four becoming hurt and enraged each time someone did not meet my expectations of what I had wanted them to be; notch five, unrequited worry and angst over how I was going to function in life with people at the center.

Coming to understand my journey as a martyr did not just happen on my own. It came with the help of other voices and, most importantly, the loving voice of my Heavenly Father. They were able to point out my blind spots, and sometimes other people are needed to help point these out. Pointing out these blind spots should not be done in hostility or meanness but in love and in the understanding that there is more potential for our lives than where they currently are. This is why it is important to guard your circle of influence and make sure the voices speaking into your life are ones that are going to speak the truth and hope of Jesus.

Going back to my realization at the top of the hill, I stood and looked at the journey I had taken over the last several months (or even years), and I instantly wanted to beat myself up and enter another destructive cycle, shame. I remembered how lonely being at the top of the hill was and how angry I had gotten that other people had not joined me (silly, I know). However, as I looked again, I could see another figure climbing the hill, and this was a figure I had been very familiar with since I was a small child. This figure was the Man I had known and walked with since age four. This Man was Jesus. Here He climbed, with His arms extended, ready to take me down from a hill I had gotten myself onto. He had been waiting for me for a long time, but God is a gentleman and does not force new life choices or healthier decisions. Instead, He waited until I reached the point where I had hit a place I did not want to be, until I acknowledged the true depth of the problem and, my complete need for Him. Then, He climbed up to meet me at the top of my hill and extended His loving hands of grace and mercy to help. The next and honestly most critical part of my journey was taking the hand of Jesus and allowing Him to lead. I spent much of my life holding onto things that I did not need to hold onto, and it kept me from grabbing onto the hand of the One who wanted to move me forward in victory.

God wants to do the same thing for you.

When we acknowledge our plight, we look at all the baggage we carry around with us. If this journey is a hike, I cannot even imagine how much my backpack would weigh due to all of the worries and fears in it. Acknowledgement of the plight also means an acknowledgement of what we need to leave at the top of the mountain. We are not going to be able to hold Jesus' hand and hold onto all the things keeping us from living the victory Christ intends for us. So, as we acknowledge where we are, we have to make the decision to get off the hill and let go of what is keeping us from going down, with Jesus as our guide. And then, we begin to make the descent.

CHAPTER FIVE
decision to get off the hill

Have you ever had the experience of looking down from a really tall cliff or high mountain, curious as how exactly to get down? I have. If not those experiences, how about a really tall building or tall ride? For me, the feeling of being up really high is a major adrenaline rush; for others, it can incite pure terror. However, no matter what feeling it elicits in you, the top is not a place we can stay forever. We must make the choice to get down (or die up on top from dehydration and lack of nourishment).

Once, while I was in Colorado with a friend, we decided we were going to be adventurous hikers and climbed up (and I do mean up) trails and a small mountain (this is not an exaggeration). Thinking we had braved the wilderness and were truly experts of the great outdoors (yeah, right), we decided to leave trail markers (that we never found again, mind you) and set off on a crazy adventure. Though we did not know in the moment, we quickly got off the trail and ended up lost on a mountain for a solid eight hours. It felt like real Bear Grylls survival as we picked the moment we would eat our packed sandwiches while we saved the fruit and water for a more dire time. (This sounds dramatic, but I assure you it was scary.) As we trucked along, or upwards, I should say, we ended up in snow. (When we had started this little adventure, we were somewhat warm, and we had both been in t-shirts and tennis shoes. Do you know how hard it is to climb a mountain in tennis shoes?? I digress.) Much to our chagrin, we also ended up hearing bears growling in the distance. By now, what had seemed like our brilliant idea had now turned into a desperate plea to get back to civilization as quickly as humanly possible. Our shoes were soaked, and we were now getting unbearably cold and hungry. Without paying much attention to how quickly we were ascending, we had kept climbing up the mountain until we ended up almost vertical, looking back down and trying to figure out how we were going to get out of this mess we had found ourselves in. How had we not noticed we were vertical? Because the climb was slow, and the elevation and steepness had increased gradually. Plus, if we kept climbing to the top, maybe we would see the trail that would lead us to civilization. (It did not quite work out this way, but we gave it our best effort.) This mountain peak was not Mt. Everest by any stretch of the imagination, but it was a peak nonetheless. Now, with no possible trail in sight, we determined we had to make the decision to just get down, no matter what direction that took us or how it would have to be executed. Eventually, we assumed, we would hit the road and end up back toward the land where all the people were. (Is anyone else now singing *Little Mermaid* songs?) From the top, we had kind of managed to get our bearings enough to figure out where to go, but it did not go as smoothly as we would have hoped. Our off-trail climb had not happened instantly, but we still had to pay the consequences for choosing to go up a hill (or small mountain peak) we were not meant and also not prepared for. Does this sound familiar to anyone else? How many times does this happen?

Here was our decision: Either stay at the top of this really cold mountain, unable to make forward progress, or literally slide down and pray to God for our safety. (Might I also mention that our tennis shoes had very little grip, and we were slipping all over everywhere?) So, we made the decision that it was going to be best to just slide. Gently, though not gracefully, and miraculously, we ended up in a downward direction at a reasonably slow rate without taking out many trees along the way. Thankfully, we made it down from the top and traversed our way to the road (that we both literally kissed, we were so thankful to be off the mountain) eight hours after embarking on our adventure. We were wet and cold, as we had somehow managed to end up in a small creek going back down to civilization, but we had made it back to the land of the living. Getting off trail was not immediate, but even the smallest missteps veered us off course. Does this not sound like life sometimes? What starts with one small step can often lead us to unmarked territory that we were never meant to be in.

Thankfully, as with my traumatic mountain story (the pictures are really funny now), God can also help us get back down from the mountains or hills we are not supposed to be on. Sometimes, it takes a dramatic slide down that may be a little scary. Sometimes, you just have to keep going, looking for any signs that you are heading in the right direction. As followers of Christ, we can trust that He will lead us on the right path, even if it is uneven and scary. The important part of any journey is to just keep moving.

As I am sure you are gathering, getting down is not going to be a seamless process. It is full of bumps and rocky crags and sometimes gently placing one foot over the other (or sliding one inch at a time and putting your hands down to brace yourself as you descend). It is full of missteps and challenging moments, but it is also full of abundant and abounding grace. God, in His divine sovereignty and wisdom, knows that we need all the help we can get in navigating life and climbing off a hill we are not meant to be on. Thankfully, this is not a process we have to do alone, nor should we try to do it alone.

Making a decision means a course of action must follow. Decisions without action lead to wasted thought bubbles and misused energy and potential. When any form of decision is made, there often comes a sense of uncertainty or lack of completely understanding how it is all going to pan out. Standing at the top of the hill deciding to get down is a lot harder to do without a course of action for deciding how to accomplish that goal. Often, we can feel stuck and not always know the next right decision. However, as followers of Christ, we can have the assurance that any decision to lay down what He does not have for us, and pick up what He does, will allow Him the chance to lead and guide our steps.

I am reminded of the story in Exodus when Moses is telling Israel that God will deliver them out of the hands of the Egyptians. Here they are in a mess, and they are fearful of what might happen to them: Will they end up back in slavery, or will they die on the way to freedom? Moses speaks some very powerful words to them in that moment: "And Moses said to the people, 'Fear not, stand firm, and see the salvation of the Lord, which he will work for you today. For the Egyptians whom you see today, you shall never see again. The Lord will fight for you, and you have only to be silent'" (Exodus 14:13-14). I think, when we have gotten ourselves into trying situations, one of the hardest things to do is be still (or silent) and to remember that Someone far greater than any of us is working and in control. I remember being at the top of that mountain and having to take a moment to pause and survey the world around me to make sure I was not going to plummet to my death. When we are in the middle of difficulty and in acknowledgement that there is something happening that is greater than our ability to handle on our own, we have to sometimes just take a moment to pause and realize that God is in control. God is bigger than we are, and, if we are still, we can remember Who it is that is fighting our battles for us. I think being still is one of the most important things I can teach anyone that I interact with in normal life or while they are sitting in my counseling and coaching office working through tough issues.

After this harrowing mountain illustration of martyrdom, where are we on our journey? Well, there is recognition and acknowledgement of the problem of being an unnecessary martyr as we have climbed to the top of hills we are not meant to climb. There is a decision to no longer die on unnecessary hills. And we sit. And we wait. And we regain our communion with God. We lay down all the garbage we carried to the top, and we grab Jesus' hand and allow Him to help us back down. Remember the figure we saw climbing up the hill to us? Often, we have lost our communication with Jesus, which keeps us from trusting in the guiding comfort of His mighty hand. We have become so clouded by the noise around us that we have forgotten what it means to be still and linger in His presence. It will take practice and daily discipline to regain this communion, because we have conditioned our brains to be full of the noise of others' opinions or the things that must be accomplished. We have forgotten the peaceful practice of sitting with the One who restores the darkest places of our souls. So, how do we begin to sit with this elusive (though only elusive because we allow ourselves to get to that place) figure again, you may ask? We shift our focus, our perspective. We remember that He does not want to be elusive to us but wants to have a relationship with us. We begin to worship.

CHAPTER SIX
worship

We now have the determination to get off the hill and be with our King, but sometimes we want to go back to what we know is comfortable. Any form of change takes away from the sense of the familiar, and it requires much stronger willpower to keep from going back in the same direction. It takes work to keep moving down the hill until we end up on solid ground. In fact, it takes a lot of self-discipline.

In my work as a counselor, relapse is a common occurrence. Why? Because when the vat of human strength runs out, it is easy to just go right back to the patterns from before. It takes something much larger and stronger than what we naturally have to keep from going back to what is comfortable. And where does this strength come from?

Jesus and our time with Him.

One of the best pieces of advice I have ever been given is to worship when I am in a hard place. When I have been troubled or have been running around with a completely out-of-control thought life, there has never been anything more calming than putting on worship music and redirecting my mind to the King of Kings. Worship does not always have to be accompanied by music, though this is a very common practice. Worship is also about just sitting and admiring who God is and being in reverent awe of Him. Worship is a lifestyle and a choice and should be an integral part of our everyday living.

The beautiful thing about worship is that it redirects our mind away from other people and the plights we are in, and it places our mind on the Holy and Sovereign Creator. It bridges the gap between the places of hardship and the place where the Spirit of God dwells. It ushers in peace and blocks out the noise from the world. It restores our souls and chips away at the bondages we are walking in.

There is a reason Scripture places a heavy emphasis on worship. When we read of the battles between Israel and neighboring enemies, we see that the first people sent into the battlefield are the musicians, the worshippers (2

Chronicles 20:21). When we worship, our brains are engaging in what they are created to do, the divine purpose of being in communion with God. Worship gets our minds centered. Without a centered mind, we will never be able to win the battle. We will never be able to get ourselves off the hill. We will never be able to move forward into the victorious life God creates for us. Without worship, we cannot get our eyes on the One who wins our battles for us.

Worship does something the world does not encourage; it takes our minds off ourselves. The enemy wants us to spend a lot of time thinking about "me" when God wants us to spend our time thinking about Him. Is this because we serve a narcissistic God? No, this is because He knows that in Him is where our peace is found, because we are created to be in direct communication with God. Our egocentric minds have a hard time shifting the focus from ourselves to the One who deserves all the attention. Especially in western culture, we are taught to look out for number one instead of looking to the only Number One.

Our communion with God was first broken when sin entered the world, when Adam and Eve ignored the

Word of God and did things their own way. As a self-inflicted martyr, I spent a lot of time doing things my own way. I held onto things and circumstances I was not supposed to hold onto (as was alluded to in the battle armor story); I worried about things that were not mine to worry about. All along, God was asking me to walk in the garden with Him and allow Him to carry the heavy load.

It is not our responsibility to fix everyone's thoughts, feelings or emotions, nor is it our responsibility to make everyone love us. It is, however, our responsibility to nurture our relationship with God day in and day out. It is our responsibility to engage in worship and to direct our hearts and our minds to the Savior of the world. It is our responsibility to relinquish the identities we are not supposed to carry and carry the mantra of being a child of God. When you know who you are, it makes it much easier not to climb hills you are not meant to climb. How do we know who we are? We spend time with Him. We worship.

Worship is not just singing songs or listening to music (though those are both great and important). Worship is a lifestyle of centering our thoughts on God. We worship what we think about the most; that is why we have many modern-day idols in our world. People worship social media or text messages or phones or people or jobs, and then they walk around with a void in their hearts, not understanding why they cannot move forward with healthy mindsets and attitudes. So, where should our thoughts go? I think you are probably catching on here, Jesus. We worship what we think about the most, and I want to think about Jesus more than anything or anyone else.

I have worshipped people and their opinions of me. I have worshipped how I made other people feel and how they made me feel. I have even worshipped replaying situations and negative moments in my head. Sometimes, the enemy still tries to lure me back into those traps. The moment I shifted my worship to the correct place, however, I recognized God was with me. I was able to take His hand and keep walking down the hill. He caught me when I fell and grabbed my chin when my eyes began to drift. As I worshipped, He made His presence very known. He illuminated the things that were keeping me blocked from Him. That is an amazing and indescribable gift.

Allow me to jump back to this concept of identity. I am going to be so bold as to say the type of martyrs we are discussing in this book do not have their identities in the right place. Tasks, people, careers, spouses, children, homes, status, prestige and other things can very often mire even the best of Christ-followers in the shifting sands of unstable identity. Who we are is very different from who we serve in our day-to-day lives, what we do or our general status in life. When we forget this very poignant reality, we climb hills we are not meant to climb and die on hills God never meant for us to die on. Who we are meant to be is found in one simple place, the Cross of Jesus Christ. Our identity was forever sealed when Jesus took the punishment for our sins and sealed our place as children of God. And that, my friends, is the only stable, unshifting ground we will ever be able to anchor ourselves in. We are children of God, and that is the only solid identity any of us will have for the rest of our lives. Status may change, relationships may change, jobs may change, but who God is, and who He says we are, never changes.

If we do not know who we are, and WHOSE we are, we will never be able to recognize that the battles we are fighting may not be ones that we are meant to fight. Why have we spent so much time focusing on worship? Because it is in the presence of the King that we discover who we are, no matter how many times we need to be reminded of that truth. It is where we discover our true weapons of warfare and find peace to get down from an unnecessary hill we probably never meant to end up on in the first place. It is where we lay down the weapons we were never meant to carry and gird ourselves with the assurance that the battle has already been won. It is where we lay down the identities we were never meant to carry and pick up the one given to us over 2,000 years ago on Calvary.

Now that we have worshipped, how do we continue to deepen our communion with God and further solidify this identity in Christ? We pray. And we pray without ceasing.

CHAPTER SEVEN
prayer

Prayer is a very vital part of not only Christian practice but also of successful Christian living. It is a two-way street that requires speaking with God AND listening for the voice of the Father. I can sense a palpable difference in the times when I am more connected to God through prayer and times when I am not. One of my favorite verses in Scripture is Jeremiah 29:13, which says, "You will seek me and find me, when you seek me with all your heart." This comes directly after God tells the Israelites that He has plans to prosper them and give them hope and a future while they are in the middle of exile. These words did not come at a time in Israel's history that was pleasant. In fact, this was a time of desperation and heartache. They were removed from their promised land and in the hands of an enemy. The Israelites got themselves to this place with their disobedience, and we get ourselves on top of hills the same way. As the Israelites learned, their redemption, their restoration, came when they got their eyes fully back on God. We must do the same. For some of us, this is a lesson we tend to have to learn repeatedly.

Seeking God is not a practice that returns void. God is not interested in a divine game of hide and seek, where we count to 10 and hope He is able to find us in whatever closet we are camped out in. If you want to find Him, He will present Himself to you. Too often we think we cannot hear or see God or that He does not want to be found by us. There are periods when God does not give us a direct answer, or we have to wait to hear His voice. However, this does not mean that He does not commune with us. It just means He understands that when our minds are focused on Him and in pursuit of Him only, the distraction and difficulty of being somewhere we do not want to be begins to fade in His presence. Sometimes, it requires patience and actually WAITING on the Lord. Our instant society does not lend much time to lingering and being still, but as we alluded to earlier, it is oh, so important.

I have a prayer that I have repeated to myself several times over the last several months, and it goes like this: "Lord, help me to live a Spirit-empowered life. Help me to see, not with the lens of my flesh, but the lens of my Spirit. Help me to remember that you have this, heal the brokenness, and allow me to let go." I repeat this in varied forms to myself all the time. Why does the Bible tell us to pray without ceasing? I do not believe we do this practice because God needs us to nag Him in order to get an answer, but rather in acknowledgement that the more we direct our attention to God, the more we find solace in His arms. This prayer has transformed my life, and I have repeated it over and over so that it became ingrained. When the enemy wants me to start climbing another hill, I pray this prayer, and I remember the lessons the Lord has already so gently and powerfully spoken to me. I remember the goodness of God. I remember that climbing off the hill was a new way of living for me, and God was going (and continues still) to have grace with me. It becomes automatic and the thing that takes up space in my brain instead of the worry or the fear that wanted to creep in before. It allows my feet not to start another unnecessary climb.

I love Dr. Caroline Leaf, and I have for years. The woman is brilliant, and I am convinced that any book I write will discuss some of the aspects of her work. She speaks repeatedly to the biblical principle that what we think about the most grows within us. If I am sitting and thinking about things that are in direct contradiction to the things of God, that is what will grow, and that is what will invade my head space. If I continue to direct my attention toward divine communion and holy interaction, this will be the thought that pervades. Getting off the hill through worship and prayer takes intentionally breaking down the thoughts that we have wired into us (worry over others' feelings, opinions, being a slave to tasks and more) and replacing them with the truth of who God is and who God says we are. God designed us to live in peace; we just have to choose it.

Now, please do not get the idea that I am a monk who prays 24 hours a day, seven days a week. I have not hit that spiritual height, nor will I even begin to pretend that I am anywhere close. I still enjoy being with people and going out and interacting with the world around me. I have just come to the understanding that I am not going to get off the hills I find myself on through any other means than

Jesus Christ. I know that I have to have directed, intentional time every day to sit with my Master. If I do not create the space for this, I feel it, and I do not like how it feels. Being with Jesus is transformative.

Prayer has a really good way of getting my mind off unnecessary difficulties and places my eyes directly on Jesus. It is a gift and a gift I am thankful I can take full advantage of. It saddens me that it took me so long to understand how life-giving prayer is, but now that I have tasted it, I do not ever want to let it go. Prayer is just as life-giving as anything else in our lives. It amazes me how we aggressively treat cancers or serious health concerns, yet we let our spiritual lives decay. We do not understand that we need our connection with God to live full, abundant lives, to be as healthy mentally and emotionally as we are physically. Far too often, we let ourselves experience spiritual death, and we do not take it nearly as seriously as we should.

I do not think Christians always fully understand the true grace of God present in the fact that we get to directly speak with Him every day. Before Jesus' ultimate sacrifice, Jews had to talk to a priest, who would then talk to God on their behalf. We do not have to do that anymore. When

Jesus died, that veil was torn in two, and we now have direct access to the Father. We get to sit with Him day in and day out. We get to invite Him to continue to climb on the hills we have found ourselves on and allow Him to help us get back down. We get to take His hand and let Him lead us home. What a gift. What an indescribably beautiful gift.

CHAPTER EIGHT
more worship and more prayer

What more could I possibly have to say on the
topics of worship and prayer? I think we understand that
both are really important. However, in my work as a
counselor, I have quickly come to realize that people need
repetition. How do we learn something? We learn by doing
it over and over again.

Why do I want to spend so much time emphasizing
worship and prayer? Because I know this is the only place
where we truly rediscover who we are and who we are
meant to be. It is the only place where the healing balm of
Jesus can continually sweep over our souls and remind us
of the freedom we have in Him. Yes, there is healing in the
conversations we can have with other people, but nothing
soothes and refreshes the soul like time in the presence of

Jesus.

When people are really seeking answers or direction from the Lord, they often will enter a period of fasting and prayer. Sometimes they will fast from eating meals, drinking pop, watching TV or something else. The purpose of a fast is to give something up (typically food because the lack of food has a pretty strong effect on us) so that we can experience God's presence in a deeper and richer way. Sometimes fasting is pursued for specific answers, but it can also simply bring us into deeper communion with God.

However, I often fear that we can be trapped into the cycle of only really seeking God at specific times of the year. Churches will often do fasts at the beginning of the year to allow God to truly direct them as they go into a new beginning. There is nothing wrong with this, but our pursuit of Jesus should be a daily decision. Worship and prayer should not just be something we do on Sundays and Wednesdays (or whenever a specific Bible study time is happening), and, too often, it can become that way.

I have fallen into this pattern more often than I would like to admit. It would be really easy for me to just spend time with God when I was at church or doing church-related activities. I remember going to church camp as a kid and receiving the "high" that would come from being in God's presence for a solid week, only to return to a normal routine. I forgot that God wanted to meet with me every other time of the year just as much as He wanted to during my intentional times of seeking Him. And why were my only intentional times of seeking during those specific times?

Church camps and fasting are both GREAT things that we can (and should) participate in. God has done some amazing miracles in my life while I was engaged in one or both of those activities, and I am grateful for those moments. My heart is to simply convey that those cannot be the only times we pursue Jesus. We must pursue Him every moment of every day. We must enter into His presence through the reading of His Word, prayer and worship.

We have every excuse imaginable not to spend time with God: tiredness, craziness of work, children, endless responsibilities and other things. These are all important, and they are all very time-consuming. I have yet to be married and have children, so I do not fully understand the struggle it would be to pursue my relationship with God and juggle a family. However, I believe that God brought me to a place where I deeply understood how much of a life source it is for me to engage daily with Him. Sometimes my prayer times are longer, and sometimes they are shorter, and I believe Jesus has grace with us when we are in seasons that are just flat difficult. I am not trying to put anyone on a guilt trip here. My heart is to remind us all that we need Jesus every moment of every day. Maybe that means putting on worship music with screaming children in the back seat or allowing ourselves a moment of prayer when we jump in the shower. Whatever it looks like, we must make time. We will always find time for the things that are truly a priority for us.

When we begin to look at time with Jesus as the very act of sustaining our lives, it makes its relevance a lot more powerful. I am not saying there are not struggles in etching out daily time, and I know everyone has to find their own groove and their own routine. However, if we are ever going to be successful at climbing down unnecessary hills or fighting other snares the enemy tries to lay before us, we have to know Jesus. The only way we fully know Him is by spending time with Him.

This does not mean that it will always be easy or that we will not have temptations or obstacles to overcome.

What it does mean is that we will have such a connection with our Heavenly Father that when hard moments come, we can draw on the Scriptures that we have meditated on; we can linger on the precious words He has spoken to us; we can draw solace from the hope we have when we linger in His presence. We can know, no matter the hill or the struggle, Jesus will always be on our side.

I am always in awe when I go to other countries and observe how they live life. When I went to Honduras, the people were in no rush. They came to church and stayed until they had met with God. They lingered in His presence and enjoyed fellowship with Him and other believers. I am a "rusher" by nature and have a very hard time lingering anywhere. I want to get in and get out, and this is often how I have treated my relationship with God. "Okay, Lord, I am here for my quick fix, and now I will be on about my day." I wonder how much heartache I would have saved myself if I had allowed my relentless pursuit of Him to be what took up all my energy for all of my life. Of course, I realize that we are all human, and we do live busy lives. I merely wonder what life would look like if we left more margin for the Spirit of God to move. What kinds of miracles would we experience? What kinds of hills would we be able to climb down faster?

Again, I do not pray all day. In fact, I am not anywhere near where I would like to be in my relationship with God, and that very fact makes me want to keep pursuing Him even more. However, I notice the very tangible difference when I have allowed my pursuit of other things (the opinions of others, worry over the potential loss of relationships, holding onto everything with the tightest grip imaginable, being a slave to my own plan) to overshadow my pursuit of Jesus. I notice when the anxiety begins to flare and when I have not allowed myself the opportunity to just sit with Him. Do I often want to rush to the next thing or make sure I am always a part? Yeah, I do, but then I hear Jesus gently remind me that it is with Him that I find my peace.

Since a young age, I have always wanted to be a part of the action. My mom had the hardest time getting me to take naps when I was little because I was truly afraid that I was going to miss out on all the fun. I was afraid that life would happen without me. This desire not to be alone was another of the steps I took toward becoming an unnecessary martyr, and it led me to a life with a lack of peace. Even as an adult, I can often let other things or the desire to be with people distract me from sitting with Jesus. I do not want to miss out on moments, so I can easily take away moments of being with the Source of life. And, you know what I have realized? I do not experience those moments with others like I should. My worry and fear over how others perceive me often gets carried into my interactions. Why? Because I was too busy worrying about being in the action instead of being with the One who makes all the action worthwhile. I did not spend nearly enough time with Jesus.

For you, it may be the next task that needs to be accomplished. It may be hard to sit down and spend that time with God because you are a martyr to the to-do list you have created for yourself. You may think that if you do not get it done, no one will, or there are just too many things that have to happen in a day. We all have busy lives, but what if we considered the reasons we do any of what we do? What if we ceased our striving and sat with the One who makes our tasks worthwhile? What if we climbed off the hill of sacrificing ourselves to things God never asked us to sacrifice ourselves to? What if we took a moment to sit in His presence to discern what activities He really wanted us to be a part of? Maybe, just maybe, we would experience life to the fullness that Jesus intended.

My favorite, King David, has this to say about time with God: "You make known to me the path of life; in your presence there is fullness of joy; at your right hand are pleasures forevermore" (Psalm 16:11). This whole Psalm is a testimony to what life with God truly brings. Remember my first discussion of some of those modern-day idols earlier in the book? If I may, allow me to share a few more: technology, social media, relationships, money, television, Netflix and others. An idol, as a reminder, is anything that receives our worship or our attention. Over the course of my life, I have spent way more time staring at a television screen or my phone than I have in the presence of God. We worship what our attention is devoted to. None of the aforementioned things are bad in and of themselves, but they can be when they replace relationship with God. We can have all the excuses in the world, but it is important to evaluate what our lives are reflecting.

Again, I do not execute any of this perfectly. I am human, and I am learning. I enjoy watching shows and movies, and I enjoy the benefits of technology and being able to go places. Doing a task and doing it well is something that is extremely admirable. God is just teaching me that none of this will fulfill me like He does, and it cannot take the place of being with Him. I will never be able to get down (or stay off) unnecessary hills without Him. Technology and Netflix will not heal my soul; only Jesus will.

CHAPTER NINE
keep making the change

The reason I have titled this chapter as I have is because sometimes it takes a while to get a new pattern, a new way of functioning, ingrained. We have to keep intentionally learning new and healthy habits and implementing new and healthy habits. As I mentioned previously, this means repetition. This means directed, intentional focus. We cannot let up. Just as another reminder, we must make the daily decision to pursue Jesus with all that we have. There is no idle time when we are about the Kingdom of God. If your mind is filled with the things of God and worship and prayer, it is going to be much harder to slip into the world of unnecessary martyrdom. Does this mean there will not be temptation? Of course not. Temptation is a part of life. However, there will also be the newfound ability to keep walking on level ground, avoiding the next hill at all costs.

Intentionality is a large part of anyone's healing process. I remember looking down the mountain with my friend and realizing I had to be VERY intentional about the steps I took and the moves I made, or I would quickly fall to my doom. In recovery, we must also be very intentional. If we do not want to fall, we have to watch where we are looking and where we are stepping.

When you have made the decision to acknowledge your plight and get off the hill, Satan will come at you hard. I do not say this to discourage you, but to help you come to the understanding that true life change is a lot of work. Every possible misstep you could make, every failure you could have, can easily come to the surface. Like a baby learning how to walk, there will be moments of tripping and stumbling over ourselves. Letting go of a life of martyrdom will not always be a simple process, but it can always be assessed from the posture of worship and prayer.

It is much easier to just let the mind aimlessly wander. When we have been in a destructive lifestyle, it takes a while to step outside of that mindset and continually make the right choices. This is not because God does not love us or wants us to fail, but because, I firmly believe, God understands we need to learn how to live the way He meant for us to live.

I had a conversation with one of my dear friends about the topic of letting something go. I was observing a situation that was really disconcerting, but I had absolutely no authority to do anything about it. So, I stewed, and I worried, and it made me a person I did not really want to be. That is the other tricky part about being an unnecessary martyr; it takes away from the person Jesus intended us to be. We were never meant to be people plagued by worry or fear or doubt or anxiety, but climbing these hills takes us to that place. Honestly, being a martyr made me try to assume some God-like responsibility, and that is not a role anyone is meant to have. That is a very humbling confession, but awareness of the enemy's tricks helps us to keep moving forward making better choices.

So, as I discussed with my friend the healing I had experienced in this particular arena, I asked her for wisdom about how to keep letting go of that which I was not supposed to hold onto. Here are some of the things she told me to do, and I hope they can be an encouragement to you, wherever you are in your journey:

1.   *Have grace for other people.*

Sometimes, when we have been a martyr on a hill, we can enter into relationships that are not necessarily the healthiest. We can worry about things that we are meant to surrender at the feet of Jesus, and we can continue to fight battles we were not meant to fight. What is the end result when people are not responding the way we think they should or we are constantly worried about offending them? It skews our view and keeps us from seeing people the way God intended us to see them.

2.   *Embrace where things are.*

I do not mean this to say that we accept unhealthy or negative situations, and my friend did not mean this either. Sometimes, when we have recognized something as unhealthy, the only chance we have to surrender is to embrace what is. If we delude ourselves into thinking that we can be the one that changes things all on our own, we never leave room for the healing, saving power of the Holy Spirit. God wants our eyes on Him, and it is hard to do that when we are constantly worried about everything else around us. This does not mean we have to stay in unhealthy situations or around unhealthy people; that is not God's design for us, either. What it does mean is that we are honest enough with ourselves about where things have ended up that we can see the way to get them to where God wants them to be.

3.   *Have grace for yourself.*

One of the hardest things for me has been having grace for myself. When I first discovered the hill I had found myself on, I expected that I would have all the answers figured out right away, and that is not the way life works. When I had not achieved the healing I wanted right away, I would get angry with myself and enter into another destructive cycle: self-degradation (or shame, as was alluded to earlier). However, this sweet friend reminded (and continues to remind) me that it is okay that we are beginners at things, and we have to keep learning things one step at a time.

If you have not read the book *The Next Right Thing* by Emily P. Freeman, I encourage you to do so. The whole premise of this wonderful read is based on how we make biblical decisions. My brief synopsis will not give it the credit it deserves, but it really is such a beautiful way to look at decision making. One of the chapters talks about giving ourselves the space to be a beginner. Whether it is launching a new business endeavor or something else, we have to give ourselves the grace to learn. When climbing down from the hill of unnecessary martyrdom, the same concept applies. We have to have grace with ourselves, and we have to learn that it is okay to start from ground zero. When we start at ground zero, we get to lay the right foundation instead of the wrong one that had dictated our lives for all these years. Then, we can really continue to let it all go.

CHAPTER TEN
surrender

As mentioned earlier, humans like control. We like to know that we have a say in our lives. When we hear words like "submit" and "surrender," our skin begins to crawl. Why? Because surrender means we let go of the trust we have in ourselves alone. This may be a harsh reality, but submitting means we have to let go of our self-trust and put our hope in the infallible Heavenly Father.

When we think of surrender in militant terminology, it is not always deemed a positive thing. If you are the one doing the surrendering to an enemy, it is not a pleasant experience. In fact, it generally means you have lost the battle. However, surrendering to the Lord means we have made the choice to ultimately win. We have made the choice that our lives are much safer in His hands than they are in our own. We are not surrendering to an enemy; we are surrendering to our Savior, whose ultimate plans and purposes are far greater than anything we could plan for ourselves.

Too often, we spend our lives surrendering to the enemy, and we do not even realize it. We want our lives to be full of peace, but we have ended up in enemy territory on more than one occasion. What is worse, we have allowed ourselves to stay there, plagued by fear, doubt, anxiety and worry. When I am experiencing anything opposite of a fruit of the Spirit (love, joy, peace, patience, kindness, goodness, faithfulness, gentleness and self-control), I know that I have landed myself in a place I should not be. However, when we surrender to God, we can trust that He is not out to destroy us, and we can trust that He is for our ultimate good.

For the longest time, I struggled to truly surrender my life to Jesus. I have always believed He is good, but I had some serious moments of questioning what He was doing and if I could really trust Him to take care of me. I can remember the moment God asked me if I was really ready to surrender, right before I turned 30, but He did it in a way that showed me how I had been living my life before.

I remember Him asking me if I wanted to live my 30s the same way I had lived my 20s, and it made me stop dead in my tracks. I have always loved the Lord, but I had a very hard time letting go of control. In that moment, it almost felt as if the Lord showed me a highlight reel of my attempts to do it my own way and how much it had been a detriment to me. All my sideways energy focused on other people, all my worry, all my desire to control, had brought me to a place where I did not want to be, at the top of a very messy hill. However, I remember the moment of sitting on my bed telling God, "Okay, I am done now. I do not like how this is going, and I really need you to help save me from myself." And, you know what? He did. Was it always an easy and simple process? No, but it was one filled with His grace and promises of hope and healing. Every step, every turn, every nudge, every step down, He was there, and He never let up or let go. That is the God we serve, and that is how much He cares.

One of my favorite quotes is from a man named Hudson Taylor, and it says this: "Christ is either Lord of all, or He is not Lord at all." This is a concept that hit me square in the face and is also backed up in Scripture (Revelation 3:16). I could not just pick and choose what areas I wanted the Lord to have. I could not hold onto my relationships with all that I had or what I thought was the best method; I had to let go, and man, was it scary. Was I really going to make the decision to make Him Lord of every part of my broken and tattered life so that He could begin the process of putting it back together?

I remember the only time I have been skydiving, and it was an exhilarating moment unlike anything I had ever experienced (this was before I made the oh-so-brilliant decision to get stuck on the top of the mountain that I shared about earlier). I went through an all-day class with a couple of friends (one of these friends being the one I got stuck on top of the mountain with), and, at the end of the training, the big moment had arrived; I got to jump out of a plane, and I was even crazy enough to jump by myself.

Now, in order to be able to pull your own chute, you have to go through hours and hours of training and certification. Thankfully, they do not just let anyone jump out of a plane alone without the proper instruction. However, they will allow you to jump solo if they pull your chute. So, here I was, a few thousand feet above the ground, hanging onto the wing of an airplane, wondering what in the world I was doing. I am an adrenaline junkie, but this was a decision I instantly regretted. I had to trust that the man who had done all my training would actually pull my chute. My friend had gone before me, and I could see that his had safely deployed. Now, it was my turn.

As the instructor counted down, I closed my eyes and finally let go. I flailed so hard letting go of that wing, and that is the exact OPPOSITE of what you are supposed to do. You are supposed to arch your back and kind of allow the air to help catch you. I did not do that; in fact, they told me they were going to use my exit from the plane as a training video on what NOT to do. However, once my chute fully inflated, I popped up and looked around at the view below. Here I was, gliding down to the ground, and it was honestly one of the most peaceful experiences I have ever had, but I would not have had it if I had not let go. My landing was not great, but I made it to the ground nonetheless. Sometimes we might bump and bob along, but God can and will bring us to a place of stopping, of rest. Sometimes our exit might not be as pretty as we would like, but He is powerful enough to help us reach the destination, even if we do not always exit in the best manner possible.

I believe God brings that back to my memory to

teach a few valuable lessons. It is okay that letting go is completely and utterly terrifying. Surrender is not always the easiest thing, but I do not think any one of us is interested in spending our lives hanging onto the wing of the plane or hanging out on top of a hill we were never meant to be on. This is not a sustainable way to live. Eventually, my hands would have gotten tired, and I would have had to find a way to let go. Eventually, you need resources from down below that cannot be found at the top of the hill. Surrender is inevitable; it is just about who you choose to surrender to.

We also have all sorts of examples of the faithfulness of God when we do choose to surrender. Scripture is chock full of all sorts of beautiful examples of surrender and obedience: Abraham surrendered his only child, Isaac, and God restored his child to him (Genesis 22), Joshua surrendered his fears to lead his people into the Promised Land (Joshua 1), Esther surrendered her safety to keep her people safe (Esther) and Paul surrendered his pious notions of who Jesus really was (Acts 9), just to name a few. The ultimate example of surrender that we have is that of Jesus. In the moment He died on that cross, He momentarily gave up His divine power to take on the sinful nature of all of mankind. He surrendered His right to be the only heir so that we could be co-heirs with Him. Surrender is not easy, but surrendering to Jesus leads to freedom. If the Savior of the world laid it all down, we should be willing to do the same thing in return.

When I watched my friend jump out of the plane and have his parachute deploy, I had an example go before me that this could work, and I really would be okay. I was not going to plummet to my death (barring anything crazy happening). The Bible gives us these examples and so many more. We have proof that God is who He says He is and that we can trust when He asks us to live our lives surrendered to Him. We have people around us who can testify to the hope that comes from living a life submitted to the King. God knew we would need constant reminders and examples, and in His kindness and faithfulness, He offers those to us. What a beautiful gift.

Make the choice to walk away from the recognized places of martyrdom. For me, that has been Facebook comments (if our self-worth is based on social media, there is a huge problem), when I feel I have offended someone (whether real or not) or constantly trying to gain the affection of others. I do not have to buy everyone's love, and I have had to come to a place where I understand I am loved just because I am a child of God. I do not have to purchase all the things for all the people to make sure I stay in their good graces. Gift-giving is not a bad thing, but it becomes a problem when it replaces the security and hope we have in Jesus.

Again, I am not perfect at this. I still want people to like me and have to assess where I am all the time. However, I do not have to do this alone. As I draw near to God, He draws near to me (James 4:8). As I make the determination to walk with Him each day and not listen to the lies of the enemy, I keep moving forward and step further and further away from the hills I found myself on for years. Though the journey will not be over until I reach heaven, I know that with Jesus by my side, I can keep fighting the good fight of faith.

CHAPTER ELEVEN
fight the good fight of faith

I would be remiss to not mention the climate of the world as I write this book. I have never experienced such discord, division and hatred as I have for the last several months in the United States. Political and racial tensions, along with a raging pandemic, have left the world bobbing on its axis and very uncertain about the future. So, why am I choosing to mention this now? Because we must do the same things I have mentioned throughout the course of this book: pray, worship, be in the presence of Jesus and acknowledge what we do and do not have control over. The hill of desiring to control what we do not have control over is one we must always climb down from.

So, where have we arrived? Hopefully at the base of what was once a very scary hill and now in the loving and comforting arms of Jesus. I wish I could tell you that you will never feel the temptation to climb another unnecessary hill again. I wish I could tell you that Satan would leave you alone, and you would never be tempted with this again. While I believe the transformative power of Jesus is WAY stronger than anything else that may come our way, we still live in a sin-stained world, and we still have to make the choice to keep living our lives honoring our King. How can we keep moving forward?

We keep moving forward with constant awareness, constant acknowledgement of the love of Jesus, constant hope in His saving arms, constant prayer, constant worship and a constant surrender of our lives to the hands of Jesus. We move forward by making time for the Lord daily, making Him the true and only Lord of our lives (not relying on ourselves) and making the decision that NOTHING is more important than that time with Him. When we make mistakes or hurt other people, we apologize, learn from our actions, and move forward. Too often, we can find ourselves in different traps, and not being able to let go of the past is a common trap for us all.

Nature has always had a way of helping me gain perspective, and it is a perspective that continues to help me as I keep fighting the good fight of faith. It is often ocean scenes that the Lord will draw my mind toward when I am having a moment of chaos, and I jump at any opportunity I have to be at the beach. There is something about watching the power of the ocean that is really calming. I can sit and hear the tides come in and out and be reminded of the great workings going on in that water. There is a whole other ecosystem that exists, and it is one I cannot even fully comprehend. The same being who created the tides, the ecosystems and the ocean waves holds me in the center of His hands, helping me to keep moving forward no matter the snares that try to entrap me.

During the last season of my life when God was helping me climb back down a martyr hill, my mind would often picture a beach at sunset. I live in the middle of Kansas, so beaches and mountains are not things I get to experience often. However, I do get to witness the most beautiful sunsets. My mind would combine this beautiful sunset view with the idea of being on a beach, walking hand-in-hand with my Savior. When I looked back at the journey the Lord had taken me on, I could see the chains that had fallen off me, cut by the truth of who God is and who He says I am. I am not one that often receives visions, and that may just be a me issue, but when I do, I treasure them in my heart for always. I write them down so I do not forget. Do not ever forget how faithful God has been in your life. When the enemy tries to tell you there is nothing left to fight for, remember how faithful He has been and will always be.

I think the beauty of these visions and of being at the ocean is the perspective it can provide. The ocean is extremely vast and covers over 70% of the earth. When I look at this deep expanse, I am reminded that my small corner of the world is just as cared for as the workings of that ocean. I remember being on a trip to the east coast to visit one of my dear friends, and she was kind enough to allow me to be at a beach at the end of December. It was freezing cold, but seeing a real-life example of what God had so faithfully shown me over the six months prior was a reminder that Jesus sees, Jesus knows and Jesus has me.

I think we can often have the misconception that once we have "healed," there is no more work to be done. I would strongly disagree with that statement. We are all still fallible beings in constant need of the redemptive work of Jesus Christ. Romans 12:2 talks about the process of renewing our minds, which leads me to believe that this is an ongoing process, an ongoing choice of surrendering and redirecting our minds. Now that we have gotten off the hill, we will have to make daily choices to not go back.

Satan knows what he is doing, and while I do not ever want to give him too much credit, he is incredibly cunning. In Ephesians 6, we see the description of the full armor of God in aiding us in our conquest to be the best disciples of Christ we can be. In verse 16, it talks very specifically about the flaming arrows that come from the enemy. Roman battle gear was no joke, and our Christian battle gear should always be on. There are no "slack" days in the Kingdom of God. 1 Peter 5:8 says we need to "be sober-minded. Your [our] adversary the devil prowls around like a roaring lion, seeking someone to devour."

So, what do these descriptions of how our enemy works invoke in me? They invoke in me the strong sense that I must be vigilant every moment of every day in my walk with the Lord. If I put my shield down for one moment, an arrow can come my way. If I let my thoughts wander away from the truth of who God is and who He says I am, the devil can come and destroy like a roaring lion. God gave me the reminder that though Satan likes to roar as a lion, Jesus is the Lion of Judah, and nothing can defeat Him. There is a reason Scripture says there is a battle, and this is a battle for souls, hearts and minds. We have the full potential to live as conquerors for the Kingdom of God, but we must stay alert. We must find our rest in His presence.

Now, please do not read this as Emily telling you to never have any fun in your life or to live in fear. Being vigilant in God's Kingdom brings an overwhelming sense of peace, and I firmly believe that God would like for us to enjoy the life He has given us. What I am implying is that when we are following the right Commander-in-Chief, we trust that He will lead us into victory. We trust that we can rest in His presence and have assurance that He will help us to prevail. Walking with Christ is the most life-giving choice we will ever make, but we also have to be aware of the sin-soaked world in which we live. To be negligent in our pursuit of Christ is to sacrifice the peace and joy that comes in journeying day in and day out with Him. In other words, we will not like the results if we neglect our pursuit.

As with any journey that we encounter in our lives, once we get off the hill, we have to make the choice to keep moving in a direction away from the hill. The further we are from the hill, the easier it is not to want to climb back up. We must keep praying. We must keep worshipping. We must keep surrendering. We must keep trusting. We must keep asking ourselves who God says we are, and what is it He wants us to do for His Kingdom. Even when we do have moments of temptation or we take a few missteps, the gentle conviction of the Holy Spirit can help us course correct and get us back on track.

Another interesting note: As we keep fighting and moving forward on our journeys of faith, we must have grace for others as the Lord has had grace for us. Once I gained awareness of the hill I had ended up on and had made active steps to start climbing down and stay down, I had moments of finding it difficult to be gracious with others. When our struggles look the same as other people's, it is easier to extend a loving arm. However, when they struggle differently, it can be a little bit more difficult to be as gracious as the Lord wants us to be. (At least, that has been my own personal experience.)

Climbing down the hill and moving forward in the freedom God has given us should be a journey that leads us to having the utmost compassion for others, but for me and for a short time, it honestly made me angry. It made me angry that other people could not see the hills they were on or the struggles they were having in their own lives. It made me angry that they were not willing to change. Why did this make me angry? Because I still wanted to fix it. I still wanted to have some level of control. I had forgotten that I am meant to be broken over sin, and righteous anger is nowhere even close to the fleshly kind. While I had gotten off the hill of martyrdom, I was keeping myself tied to it by allowing myself to be angry instead of genuinely broken for the hurt I was witnessing. I had a season where I let my healing inflate me instead of truly humble me, and that is not healing, that is pride. There is a reason pride is one of the seven deadliest sins; its consequences can be devastating and far-reaching.

When we get off the hill, we have to remember that we ourselves need the saving love and power of Jesus. No one could make us get down; no one could change our minds, so may we all pray to have the same compassionate and loving lens as Jesus has with us. Sin and brokenness are difficult, and they impact every arena of our life. But, as we looked to Jesus as He climbed the hill to meet us where we were, let us look to Jesus again as we pray for the people in our spheres of influence and in our communities. May our healing continually lead us to a place of humble submission as we realize it is only by the grace of the Lord Jesus Christ. If it were not for Him, we would still be trapped on a hill. The enemy wants any angle he can get, so we must keep our eyes directed squarely on our Lord and Savior. We must keep our hope and our eyes on Him so that we can see the world around us as He wishes us to see. Let us share the hope we have with those around us.

If you have found yourself trapped in a life of unnecessary martyrdom, I am right there with you, friend. However, there is freedom, and that freedom is found in none other than Jesus. Acknowledge where you are, and really give yourself the space to be honest with yourself. No one experiences true healing by trying to fake themselves out of believing there is a problem. You do not heal if you are not real. Through it all, keep those eyes on Jesus. The best place you will ever find yourself to be is in His presence. As the Psalmist says in Psalm 46:10, we can "be still and know that [He] is God."

Start taking those steps. Look around at the view and determine if it is a view, you are comfortable with. If not, invite Jesus up the hill, surrender, and let Him help you journey back down. Have grace with yourself in the process, as anything new takes time and the willingness to grow. As you ebb and flow, find Jesus' grace ebbing and flowing with you. He is for you, and He is for your victory. One step at a time. One day at a time. May we all find our true cause in dying daily to self and walking in perfect peace with the King of Kings. May the only pursuits we ever have be those that lead us closer to Jesus.

CLOSING NOTE

I am appreciative of you taking the time to read a book that is very personal to me and to my journey of healing. It is not easy to walk through an obstacle personally, let alone share it with the entire world, so thank you for taking the time to experience my story through the pages of this book. I have a couple of closing thoughts: one for the other martyrs in the world and one for the people who journey with them.

If you are one of the other martyrs out there who struggles with being on hills you are not meant to be on, be encouraged today, and know that the words of this book ring just as true for you as they do for me. God is in the healing business and desires for us to live a life of wholeness and freedom in Him. As I mention throughout the various chapters, find people who can journey with you and encourage you as you work to climb back down the hills you are on. Be brave enough to be real with yourself, so that you can experience the victory Christ died to give you. Do not give up hope. This journey is not always an easy one, but it is one filled with the goodness and grace of God.

If you are the one who knows the martyr, I implore you, please be gracious. I wrote this book to give a firsthand look into the mindsets that come with being a martyr, to allow others to encourage their martyr friends in their own journeys. Being a martyr and dying on unnecessary hills does not just happen overnight, and I firmly believe God will take those you know through a process of healing so that they may fully learn to depend on and trust in Him. Please remember, even if you do not struggle with being a martyr, we all struggle with something, and the blood covers everything equally at the foot of the cross. Reach out to those on the hills, and let them know they are not alone. I can tell you from personal experience that those who love me enough to help me when I start climbing have significant places of impact in my life.

For all of us, I leave some of my favorite words from the apostle Paul in 1 Corinthians Chapter 9 verses 24-27:

"Do you not know that in a race all the runners run, but only one gets the prize? Run in such a way as to receive the prize. Every athlete exercises self-control in all things. They do it to receive a perishable wreath, but we an imperishable. So I do not run aimlessly; I do not box as one beating the air. But I discipline my body and keep it under control, lest after preaching to others I myself should be disqualified.."

Keep going, keep running, keep learning, keep growing. Practice the disciplines of never again climbing hills not meant to be climbed. Love those around you who may struggle to keep themselves from being a martyr. And remember, our goal is a crown that will last forever. Let us leave the hills behind and walk the peaceful road to freedom with our Savior.

ABOUT THE AUTHOR

Emily Oakley is an ordained minister with the Assemblies of God, passionate about helping individuals through the mediums of counseling, coaching and training. She has been the president, CEO and lead counselor at Rebirth Ministries Inc. in Wichita, Kansas, since 2017. She loves writing about practical topics that can help people move forward in a healthy way. In her spare time, she is a passionate Disney enthusiast and coffee connoisseur who loves traveling all over the world.